Media Arabic

T0322716

Books in the series

Media Persian
Dominic Parviz Brookshaw

Internet Arabic
Mourad Diouri

Security Arabic
Mark Evans

Media Arabic
2nd edition
Elisabeth Kendall

Intelligence Arabic
Julie C. Manning with Elisabeth Kendall

edinburghuniversitypress.com/series/emev

• Essential Middle Eastern Vocabularies •

Media Arabic
Second Edition

Elisabeth Kendall

EDINBURGH
University Press

Edinburgh University Press is one of the leading university presses in the UK. We publish academic books and journals in our selected subject areas across the humanities and social sciences, combining cutting-edge scholarship with high editorial and production values to produce academic works of lasting importance. For more information visit our website: edinburghuniversitypress.com

First published 2005
Second revised edition 2012
Reprinted 2016, 2019

Edinburgh University Press Ltd
The Tun – Holyrood Road, 12 (2f) Jackson's Entry
Edinburgh EH8 8PJ

Typeset in Times New Roman
printed and bound by CPI Group (UK) Ltd, Croydon, CR0 4YY

A CIP record for this book is available from the British Library

ISBN 978 0 7486 4495 7 (paperback)
ISBN 978 0 7486 4496 4 (webready PDF)
ISBN 978 0 7486 5541 0 (epub)

The audio recordings were produced by Mourad Diouri, University of Edinburgh.

Published with the support of the Edinburgh University Scholarly Publishing Initiatives Fund.

CONTENTS

PREFACE TO THE SECOND EDITION

The second edition updates the first edition by including over 350 new terms to cover events such as the Arab spring and the search for democracy, recent natural disasters and their aftermath, new political and military developments and the economic and financial crises. Following popular demand, the second edition now includes audio recordings of the entire contents of each chapter. There is also an index of all terms for easy reference.

USER GUIDE

To enhance your ability to recall the vocabulary and to pronounce it correctly, this book is accompanied by audio recordings of the entire contents of each chapter, recorded in both English and Arabic. The audio re-cordings can be downloaded from our website and are compatible with iPods and other devices.

To access the audio files, please follow the instructions on our website: https://edinburghuniversitypress.com/book-media-arabic-html

Audio recordings

Main features

- Each Arabic term is recorded with authentic native pronunciation at normal speed.
- Each Arabic term is preceded by its equivalent in English.
- Each chapter is recorded as a single MP3 track (the track numbers correspond to the chapter numbers, e.g. Track 01 = Chapter 1).
- The audio files can be played on a computer or transferred to an MP3 device (e.g. iPod, mobile phone, etc.), enabling you to study on the move.

Tips

- Make sure that you engage actively with the audio recordings by repeating each Arabic term during the pause.
- Pause the recording and challenge yourself to produce the Arabic word before it is announced.

INTRODUCTION

The ability to access Media Arabic – the language of printed or broadcast news items – has become increasingly important in the light of recent developments in the Middle East. Consequently, the need for a 'quick-fix' vocabulary of Media Arabic is greater than ever. Arabic dictionaries are not equipped to deal with Media Arabic, which involves many new coinages to express contemporary concepts (for example, drone, no-fly zone, financial bailout, multi-culturalism). While English-speaking students can deduce some terms from Arabic to English by thinking laterally (for example, ministerial straightening equals cabinet reshuffle, the falsification of elections equals election-rigging), this is a much more hit and miss process when attempted from English to Arabic. Until now, getting to know the Arabic for common contemporary media terminology has necessitated a long period of familiarisation with the Arabic media. This book is designed to help undergraduates, postgraduates, governmental, military, diplomatic and business personnel bypass this lengthy process.

This book aims to supply the core vocabulary of Media Arabic in a logical format to provide easy reference and easy-to-learn lists testing both Arabic to English and English to Arabic. Familiarisation with this book will furnish the reader with an invaluable knowledge of the key vocabulary components essential to comprehend, translate, write and speak contemporary Media Arabic. Whilst independently useful, this book can be used in conjunction with Julia Ashtiany's excellent *Media Arabic*, a coursebook which sets the vocabulary in context and teaches students to manipulate typical Media Arabic structures and formats.

This book comprises eight chapters, organised by topic: General; Politics and Government; Elections; Military;

Economics; Trade and Industry; Law and Order; and Disaster and Aid. The initial General chapter comprises vocabulary pertaining to reports, statements, sources and common media idioms of a general nature. Prepositions and idiomatic time expressions are listed only where particular variations arise in Media Arabic. For example, 'day', 'week' and so on are excluded whereas 'in the long term', 'in the near future' are included. Generally, basic vocabulary such as would be acquired during elementary language training is excluded. The General and Politics and Government chapters are naturally the longest, since much of this vocabulary is also used in media discussions concerning the Military, Economics, Trade and Industry and so on. Vocabulary is not repeated, except where this forms part of an expression to produce a new meaning. Expressions have been excluded where the reader has the information to assemble these logically. For example, 'intelligence' and 'military' are both supplied as general media vocabulary items in the General chapter, therefore 'military intelligence' does not feature as a separate entry in the Military chapter.

Each chapter has its own internal logic. For example, the Politics and Government chapter begins with common political acronyms and organisations followed by political systems, descriptors of political stance, political bodies and organisations, political offices and roles, geographical entities, and so on. Direct subtitles for groupings within each chapter have been avoided since not all vocabulary items can be neatly categorised beyond the broad chapter title. Within each logical grouping, alphabetical order has purposely been avoided since this has a negative impact on the learning of vocabulary lists. Lastly, this book does not claim to be exhaustive and the choice of vocabulary is necessarily to some extent subjective. However, every effort has been made to select the most useful and/or common vocabulary items, taking into account popularity calculated by using internet search engines in Arabic and linguistic frequency lists (although very commonly used words are assumed knowledge).

Notes on the formal presentation

The Arabic is vocalised to ensure correct pronunciation and entrench in the mind the vocalisation patterns of certain structures. However, short vowels are not supplied where:

- a fatha precedes a long alif or a ta' marbuta
- a kasra precedes a long ya
- a damma precedes a long waw

The pronunciation of sun and moon letters is assumed knowledge and has not been marked.

End vowels have not been supplied where they are not generally pronounced or where they vary for case.

In general, Arabic nouns are supplied in both the singular and plural; the plural is printed after the comma.

A circular ha is shown to indicate the location of the direct object in cases where a verb takes a preposition after the direct object.

Where '+ idafah' is written in the text, this indicates that the Arabic must be followed by the genitive construction.

First form verbs

These have been supplied in the form of the basic stem (past tense masculine singular) followed by the present tense (masculine singular with the middle vowel marked) and the masdar (verbal noun). The middle vowel of the past tense has only been supplied where this is not a fatha. Where two short vowels are marked with the same letter, this indicates that both are possible.

Derived forms of the verb

These have been supplied only in the form of the basic stem (past tense masculine singular), since present tense vocalisation and masdars are predictable for derived forms of the verb. The present tense and masdars have been supplied only where the spelling of the verb changes significantly (for example, the present tense of second form first radical hamza verbs), where a separate vocabulary item is intended, or where the word is commonly misvocalised.

Abbreviations

s.t.	something
s.o.	someone
pl.	plural
adj.	adjective
lit.	literally
v.i.	intransitive verb
v.t.	transitive verb
ه	direct object

1. GENERAL

وَسائِل الإعْلام	the media
الصِحافة	the press
وِكالة الأَنْباء	press agency
صَحيفة، صُحُف \ صَحائِف	newspaper
جَريدة، جَرائِد	"
صِحافيّ \ صُحُفيّ، -ون	journalist
مُحَرِّر، -ون	editor
مُعَلِّق، -ون	commentator
مُراسِل، -ون	correspondent
مُقابِل، -ون	interviewer
كاتِب عَمود، كُتّاب أَعْمِدة	columnist
مُراقِب، -ون	observer; censor
ناقِد، -ون \ نُقّاد	critic
خَبير، خُبَراء	expert
مُتَخَصِّص، -ون	specialist
عُنْوان، عَناوين	headline
مَقالة، -ات	article
اِفْتِتاحيّة، -ات	editorial
مُقابَلة، -ات	interview
الأَخْبار	the news

تِلِفِزْيون فَضائِيّ	satellite television
قَناة، قَناوات	channel
أَخْبار عاجِلة	breaking news
تَغْطية مُسْتَمِرّة	rolling coverage
تَغْطية حَيّة	live coverage
مَقْطَع فيديو، مَقاطيع فيديو	video clip
مُؤْتَمَر صُحُفِيّ \ صَحَفِيّ	press conference
مَصْدَر، مَصادِر	source
مَصادِر مُطَّلِعة	informed sources
مَصادِر مُقَرَّبة مِن	sources close to
مَصادِر مَوْثوق بِها	reliable/trusted sources
مَصادِر عالية المُسْتَوَى	high-level sources
عَدَم كَشْفِ الهُوِيّة	anonymity
قال يَقول قَوْل	to say
قِيل يُقال	it was/is said
أَضاف يُضيف إضافة	to add
واصَل	to continue
ما زال، لَمْ يَزَلْ، لا يَزال	to continue, carry on
اِسْتَطْرَد	to go on to say
ذكر يذكُر ذِكُر	to mention, recall
أَكَّد يُؤَكِّد تَأْكيد	to confirm
نفَى ينفي نَفْي	to refute, deny, repudiate

أَنْكَر	to deny
اِسْتَبْعَد	to rule out; to regard as unlikely
قَلَّل مِن	to play down
صَرَّح بِ	to state
أَعْرَب \ عَبَّر عَن	to express
أَعْلَن	to declare, announce
زعم يزعُم زَعْم	to claim
نقل يَنقُل نَقْل	to communicate, convey
أَوْرَد	to state, quote, convey
طرح يطرَح طَرْح آراءَهُ	to present one's opinions
أفاد يُفيد إفادة ه بِ	to notify, inform s.o. of s.t.
أَبْلَغ ه بِ \ عَن	to tell, inform s.o. about s.t.
أَطْلَع ه عَلَى	to tell s.o. s.t.
أَدْلَى إلَى ه بِ	to let s.o. know s.t., inform s.o. of s.t.
رأى يَرَى رَأْي \ رُؤْية	to see, regard
اِعْتَبَر \ عدّ يعُدّ عَدّ	to deem, consider
اِعْتَقَد	to believe
عَلَّق عَلَى	to comment on
أَلْقَى خِطاباً	to give a speech
أَصْدَر	to publish, issue
أَذاع يُذيع إذاعة	to broadcast

وصف يَصِف وَصْف ه ب   to describe s.t./s.o. as

أَوْضَح   to clarify

شرح يشرَح شَرْح   to explain

أَلْقَى الضَوْء عَلَى   to throw light on

صدر يصدُر صُدور   to be published

نشر ينشُر نَشْر   to propagate, spread, publicise, publish

اِنْتَشَر   to be widespread

ردّ يرُدّ رَدّ عَلَى   to respond to

أجاب يُجيب إجابة عَلَى   to answer, respond to

اِسْتَفْهَم ه عن   to inquire, ask s.o. about

سأل يسأل سُؤال   to ask

أشار يُشير إشارة إلَى   to indicate, point to

لمَح \ ألْمَح إلَى   to hint at, allude to

اِقْتَرَح   to suggest, propose

اِفْتَرَض   to assume, presume

اِفْتَرَض عَلَى ه   to impose upon s.o. s.t.

أصَرّ عَلَى   to insist on

اِسْتَعْرَض   to survey, review

حَدَّد   to define

رَكَّز عَلَى   to concentrate, focus on

شَدَّد عَلَى   to emphasise, stress

سمح يسمَح سَماح لِ بِ	to allow, permit s.o. s.t.
وَصَّى يُوَصّي تَوْصية ه بِ	to advise
أوْصَى ه بِ	"
نصح ينصَح نَصْح ه بِ	"
شاوَر	to consult
اِشْتَرَط	to stipulate
طالَب ه \ بِ	to demand, request
جَدير بالذِكْر أَن	worth mentioning is the fact that
حَذَّر ه مِن \ أَنْذَر ه بِ	to warn s.o. about
حذِر يحذَر حِذْر \ حَذَر	to be cautious, wary of
اِحْتَذَر	"
شَكّ يشُكّ شَكّ في \ بِ	to doubt, suspect
تَجَنَّب	to avoid
أشاد بِ	to praise
اِنْتَقَد \ نَدَّد بِ	to criticise
قَوَّم	to evaluate
أثار الشُكوك حَوْلَ	to raise doubts about
عِبْء الإثْبات يَقَع عَلَى	the burden of proof falls on
أَقَرّ بِ \ اِعْتَرَف بِ	to admit, confess
كشف يكشِف كَشْف ه\عَن	to expose, reveal
دلّ يدُلّ دَلالة عَلَى	to show, prove

عرض يعرِض عَرْض	to show, demonstrate
أَظْهَر	"
أَساء يُسيئ إساءة إلَى صورة	to harm the image of (+ idafah)
اِكْتَشَف	to discover
عكس يعكِس عَكْس	to reflect
كفل يكفُل كَفْل \ كُفول \ كَفالة	to guarantee
أَجْرَى اِتِّصالاً هاتِفِيّاً بـ	to make a phone call to
شارَك في	to participate in
ساهَم في	to contribute to
لعِب يلعَب لَعْب دَوْراً في	to play a role in
سَبَّب	to cause
أَنْتَج	to cause, provoke, give rise to
أثار يُثير إثارة	to provoke, incite, arouse
أَثَّر يُؤَثِّر تَأْثير	to influence
تَأَثَّر	to be influenced
أَدَّى يُؤَدّي تَأْدية إلَى	to lead to
أَسْفَر عَن	to result in
مَهَّد الطَريق	to pave the way
رجع يرجِع رُجوع إلَى	to go back to, stem from
بِسَبَب \ نَتيجة	as a result of (+ idafah)
طبع يطبَع طَبْع	to impress

اِنْطَبَع	to be impressed
بحث يبحَث بَحْث ه\عَن	to explore, investigate; to discuss
ناقَش \ باحَث	to discuss
تَبادَل	to exchange (e.g. views)
تَعاوَن	to cooperate
تَناوَل	to treat, deal with s.t.
عامَل	to treat, deal with s.o.
شمِل يشمَل شَمَل \ شُمول	to incorporate, take in, include
اِنْضَمَّ	to comprise, include
اِنْضَمَ إلى	to join
وُجْهة نَظَر، ـات نَظَر	point of view
سِياق	context
ساحة، ـات	area
مَجال، ـات	field
مِيدان، مَيادين	"
مُسْتَوَى، مُسْتَوَيات	level
طَريقة، طَرائِق \ طُرُق	method
سَبيل، سُبُل	way
وَسيلة، وَسائِل	means
وَفْقاً لِ \ نَفْلاً عَن \ طِبْقاً لِ	according to
عَلَى حَسَب	" (+ idafah)

حَسْبَما	" (+ verb)
عَلَى غِرار	in the manner of, on the pattern of (+ idafah)
ما إذا	whether
عَلَناً	publicly
في إطار	in the framework of (+ idafah)
عَلَى أَساس	on the basis of (+ idafah)
بَدَلاً مِن	instead of
بِخِلاف	other than, besides (+ idafah)
مُقابِلَ	in exchange for; in relation to, in comparison with
بِما في ذلِك	including
عَلَى صَعيدٍ آخَر	on the other hand
مِن جِهةٍ أُخْرَى	"
مِن ناحيةٍ أُخْرَى	"
مِن جانِبٍ آخَر	"
فيما يَتَعَلَّق بِ	with regard to
مِن ناحية	from the point of view of, with regard to
بِالنِسْبة لِ \ إلَى	in relation to (+ idafah)
نَظراً لِ	in view of, with regard to
في هذا الصَدَد	in this respect
وَجْه، وُجوه \ أَوْجُه	aspect, approach, standpoint

إِزاءَ	in the face of, towards
تُجاهَ	towards
لا يجِب أَن ... طالما أَن	it doesn't have to ... as long as
إِلَى حَدٍّ ما	to some extent
إِلَى دَرَجة أَن	to the extent that
عَلَى حَدٍّ سَواء	equally
مِن أَجْل	for the sake of (+ idafah)
بِفَضْل	thanks to (+ idafah)
مُجَرَّد	mere, pure (+ idafah)
مِما يَعْني أَن / بِمَعْنَى أَن	meaning that
بِفَحْوَى أَن	"
عَلَى الساحةِ الدُوَليّة	on the international stage
في مُخْتَلِف أَنْحاءِ العالَم	in various parts of the world
في كُلِّ أَنْحاءِ العالَم	all over the world
إِمْكانيّة، ـات	possibility
اِحْتِمال، ـات	eventuality, probability
مِن المُحْتَمَل أَن	it is likely/probable that
مِن المُمْكِن أَن	it is possible that
مِن الواضِح أَن	it is clear that
مِن المُنْتَظَر أَن	it is anticipated that
مِن المُتَوَقَّع أَن	it is expected that
مِن الضَروريّ أَن	it is necessary to

مِن اللازِم أَن	"
مِن الواجِب أَن	"
مِن المُسْتَحيل أَن	it is inconceivable that
لا يُسْتَبْعَد أَن	it is not inconceivable that
لا بُدَّ مِن أَن	it is inevitable/essential that
جَدْوَل الأَعْمال	agenda
مَشْروع، ـات \ مَشاريع	plan, project
خُطّة، خُطَط	plan, scheme
إعْلان، ـات	declaration, announcement
بَيان، ـات	statement, declaration, communique, manifesto
تَصْريح، ـات	statement
إشارة، ـات	indication, sign
مَعْلومات	information (Arabic pl.)
اِسْتِخْبارات	intelligence (Arabic pl.)
تَحْقيق، ـات	investigation
تَقْرير، تَقارير	report, account
تَحْليل، ـات	analysis
إيضاح، ـات	explanation, clarification
شَرْح	elucidation, explanation
تَعْليل، ـات	argumentation, justification
تَبْرير، ـات	justification, vindication

وَصْف، أَوْصاف	description
أَمْر، أُمور	matter; order
قَضية، قَضايا	issue, affair
مَسْأَلة، مَسائِل	matter, question
واقِعة، وَقائِع	occurrence, incident
حَدَث، أَحْداث	event, occurrence
سِلْسِلة أَحْداث	chain of events
مُناسَبة، ـات	occasion, opportunity
فُرْصة، فُرَص	opportunity
شَأْن، شُوُون	matter, affair
وَضْع، أَوْضاع	position
مَوْقِف، مَواقِف	position, stance
حال، أَحْوال	circumstance, state, condition
ظُروف	circumstances
مَأْزِق، مَآزِق	impasse, predicament
مَوْعِد، مَواعِد	date; appointment; deadline
ميعاد، مَواعيد	"
تاريخ، تَواريخ	date; history
مَقْصِد، مَقاصِد	aim
نيّة، نَوايا	intention
هَدَف، أَهْداف	objective
غَرَض، أَغْراض	target, goal

طُمُوح	ambition
رامٍ إلَى	aiming at
نَتيجة، نَتائِج	result
عُقْب، أَعْقاب	upshot, outcome
عاقِبة، عَواقِب	consequence, outcome
عَقَبة، ـات \ عِقاب	impediment, obstacle
تَأْثير، ـات	influence
أَثَر \ نُفُوذ	"
سَبَب، أَسْباب	cause, reason
مَبْعَث، مَباعِث	cause, factor
عامِل، عَوامِل	factor
عُنْصُر، عَناصِر	element
مُبَرِّر، ـات	justification, excuse
دافِع، دَوافِع	motive
دَوافِع	dynamics (Arabic pl.)
حَقيقة، حَقائِق	fact; reality, truth

Adjectives

سياسيّ	political
ثَقافيّ	cultural
دينيّ	religious
اِجْتِماعيّ	social
زِراعيّ	agricultural

فِكْريّ	intellectual
اِقْتِصاديّ	economic
ماليّ	financial
عَسْكَريّ	military
رَسْميّ	official, formal
غَيْر رَسْميّ	unofficial, informal
سِرّيّ	confidential
مَدَنيّ	civil
اِسْتِشاريّ	advisory
شَعْبيّ	popular
قَوْميّ	national, people's (i.e. of the people)
دُوَليّ	international
أُمَميّ	UN (adj.)
تِجاريّ	commercial
صِناعيّ	industrial; artificial
إقْليميّ	regional
مَحَلّيّ	local
مِهْنيّ	professional
إداريّ	administrative
عاطِفيّ	emotional
أساسيّ	basic

جِذْريّ	fundamental
هَيْكَليّ	structural
سَلْبيّ	negative
إيجابيّ	positive
تَفاؤُليّ	optimistic
تَشاؤُميّ	pessimistic
عَمَليّ	practical
نَظَريّ	theoretical
شَفَويّ	oral
خَطّيّ	written
فِعْليّ	factual, actual; efficient; practical
حَقيقيّ	real
واقِعيّ	realistic
عارٍ \عارية تماماً مِن الصِحّة	completely untrue
مُقْنِع	convincing
عاديّ	ordinary
مَعْني \ مُرْتَبَك	implicated, concerned, involved
جُزْئيّ	partial
واسِع النِطاق	far-reaching
شامِل	comprehensive

كامِل	entire, complete
وَطيد	firm, solid
مَضْمون	guaranteed
غَيْر مَسْبوق	unprecedented
مَعْروف حَتَّى الآن بِ	hitherto known as
شَهير \ مَشْهور	famous, well-known
بارِز	prominent
مُعَيَّن	specific
مُمَيَّز	distinct
خاصّ	special, private
عامَ	general, public
مُتَفاوِت	various
مُخْتَلِف	different
عادِل	just
مُتَوازِن	balanced
مَسْؤول	responsible
مُسيء إلَى	harmful to
مَهْزول، مَهازيل	degenerate, weak
مُفْتَعَل	spurious, forged
مُعَقَّد	complicated, complex
حَذِر	cautious
مَشْروع	legitimate

مَلْموس	tangible
مَلْحوظ	noticeable
مُهِمّ \ هامّ	important
مِحْوَريّ	pivotal
حاسِم	decisive, crucial, definitive
حَرِج	critical, crucial
خَطير	significant, grave
مُرْعِب	horrifying
آليّ	instrumental
جادّ، جِدّيّ	serious
بالِغ الأهَمّيّة	of the utmost importance
عَلَى جانِبٍ كَبيرٍ مِن الأهَمّيّة	"
في المَقامِ الأوّل	"
ذو \ ذات الاِهْتِمامِ المُشْتَرَك	of mutual significance
مُثير لِلْجَدَل	controversial
غَيْر مَقْبول	unacceptable
رَئيسيّ	main, principal
شائِع	widespread
سائِد	prevailing
رائِج	current, widespread, universal
ساحِق	overwhelming
مُتَوافِق مَع	compatible with

مُلائِم	suitable, appropriate
مُشابِه	similar

Time expressions

عَلَى المَدى البَعيد	in the long term
عَلَى المَدى القَريب	in the short term
أَسْرَع ما يُمْكِن	as quickly as possible
في أَسْرَع وَقْت مُمْكِن	as soon as possible
سابِق	former
ماضٍ \ الماضي	past
حالِيّ	present, current
جارٍ \ الجاري	current
راهِن	"
مُقبِل	future, forthcoming
قادِم	next
قائِم	existing
أَخير	recent; final
نِهائِيّ	final
وَشيك	imminent
دائِم	permanent
مُؤَقَّت	temporary, interim
خاطِف	fleeting
عَلَى التَّوالي	continuously

أَخيراً	recently; finally
قَريباً	soon
عادةً	usually
نادِراً	rarely
كَثيراً	often
أَحْياناً	sometimes
في نَفْسِ الوَقْت	at the same time, simultaneously
في المسْتَقْبَلِ القَريب	in the near future
خِلالَ	during
أَثْناءَ	"
قَبْلَ	before
قُبَيْلَ	shortly before
بَعْدَ \ عَقِبَ	after
بُعَيْدَ	shortly after
في أَعْقاب	in the wake of (+ idafah)
فيما بَعْد	subsequently
فَوْرَ	as soon as
في هذِهِ الأَثْناء	meanwhile
بِتَوْقيت جرينتش	GMT (Greenwich Mean Time)

2. POLITICS & GOVERNMENT

مَجْلِس التَعاوُن الخَليجيّ	GCC (Gulf Cooperation Council)
الأُمَم المُتَّحِدة	UN (United Nations)
الجَمْعيّة العامّة	the (UN) General Assembly
مَجْلِس الأمْن	the (UN) Security Council
الدُوَل الخَمْس ذات العُضْويّةِ الدائِمة في مَجْلِسِ الأمْن	the Five Permanent Member States of the Security Council
يونَسْكو	UNESCO (United Nations Educational, Scientific and Cultural Organization)
مُنَظَّمة الإتّحاد الأُوروبّيّ	EU (European Union)
المُفَوَّضيّة الأُوروبيّة	EC (European Commission)
مُنَظَّمة حِلْف شِمالِ الأطْلَسيّ	NATO (North Atlantic Treaty Organization)
الوِكالة الدُوَليّة للطاقةِ الذَرّيّة	IAEA (International Atomic Energy Authority)
مُنَظَّمة التَحْريرِ الفِلَسْطينيّة	PLO (Palestinian Liberation Organization)
السُلْطة الوَطَنيّة الفِلَسْطينيّة	PNA (Palestinian National Authority)
جامِعة الدُوَلِ العَرَبيّة	the Arab League
الرابِطة الإسْلاميّة	the Muslim League

مُنَظَّمة المُؤْتَمَر الإسْلاميّ	OIC (the Organisation of the Islamic Conference)
الإخْوان المُسْلِمون	the Muslim Brotherhood
المُؤْتَمَر اليَهوديّ العالَميّ	WJC (the World Jewish Congress)
الكنيست	the Knesset
جَبْهة الإنْقاذِ الإسْلاميّ	the Islamic Salvation Front
الاتّحاد الإفْريقيّ	AU (the African Union)
المُجْتَمَع الدُوَليّ	the international community
الرَبيع العَرَبيّ	the Arab spring
الشارِع العَرَبيّ	the (Arab) man on the street (lit. the Arab street)
مِحْوَر الشَرّ	Axis of Evil
مُنَظَّمة العَفْوِ الدُوَليَّة	Amnesty International
حِزْب العُمَّال	the Labour Party
حِزْب المُحافِظين	the Conservative Party
الليبراليّون	the Liberals
الحِزْب الديموقراطيّ	the Democrats
الحِزْب الجُمْهوريّ	the Republicans
اليَمين	the Right
اليَسار	the Left
الأدَوات السياسيّة	the political apparatus

تَحَفُّظ	conservatism
ليبراليّة	liberalism
تَعَدُّديَّة	pluralism
نُخْبَويَّة	elitism
تَعَدُّديَّة ثَقافيَّة	multi-culturalism
مُعاداة الساميّة	anti-semitism
رَأْسْماليّة	capitalism
اِنْتِهازيَّة	opportunism
اِشْتِراكيّة	socialism
شُيوعيَّة	communism
مَرْكسيّة	Marxism
شُموليّة	totalitarianism
إقْطاعيّة	feudalism
قَبَليّة	tribalism
نازيّة جَديدة	neo-Nazism
صَهْيونيّة	Zionism
تَطَرُّف	extremism
فِئَويَّة	factionalism
اِنْفِصاليّة	separatism
مَذْهَبِيّة \ طائفيّة	sectarianism
اِنْعزاليّة	isolationism
أُصوليّة	fundamentalism

شَعْبِيّة	populism
فَوْضَى	anarchy
حُكْم ذاتيّ	self-rule, autonomy
تَقْرير مَصيرِهِ \ ها	self-determination
حُكْم لا مَرْكَزيّ	decentralised rule
مَلَكيّة دُسْتوريّة	constitutional monarchy
مُحافِظ	conservative
مُحافِظ جَديد	neo-conservative
نُخْبَويّ	elitist
رَأْسْماليّ	capitalist
اِنْتِهازيّ	opportunist
اِشْتِراكيّ	socialist
شُيوعيّ	communist
مَرْكسيّ	Marxist
شُموليّ	totalitarian
صَهْيونيّ	Zionist
مُتَطَرِّف	extremist
اِنْفِصاليّ	separatist
عَلْمانيّ	secularist
أَساسيّ \ أُصوليّ	fundamentalist
فَوْضَويّ	anarchist
شَعْبيّ	populist

مَذْهَبِيّ / طائِفيّ	sectarian
فِئَوِيّ	factional
دُسْتُوريّ	constitutional
غَيْر دُسْتُوريّ	unconstitutional
ديموقراطيّ	democratic
غَيْر ديموقراطيّ	undemocratic
قَبَلِيّ	tribal
عِرْقِيّ	racial
مُتَشَدِّد	radical, bigot
مُتَصَلِّب	hard-line
ثَوْريّ	revolutionary
يَمينيّ	right-wing
يَساريّ	left-wing, leftist
مُحايِد	neutral
اِتِّحاد، ـات	union
رابِطة، رَوابِط	confederation, league
تَحالُف	(state of) alliance
مَجْلِس، مَجالِس	council
جَمْعيّة، ـات	society, club, assembly
شَبَكة، ـات	network
تَكَتُّل	bloc
جَبْهة، جَبَهات	front

لَجْنة، ـات \ لِجان	committee, commission, board, council
هَيْئة، ـات	board, council, commission
مُعارَضة	opposition
مُقاوَمة	resistance
حِزْب، أَحْزاب	party
حِزْب حاكِم	ruling party
خَطّ الحِزْب	the party line
جِناح، أَجْنِحة	wing
حُكومة، ـات	government
حُكومة مُؤَقَّتة	caretaker/interim government
حُكومة اِنْتِقاليّة	transition government, provisional government
حُكومة اِئْتِلافيّة	coalition government
مَجْلِس الوُزَراء	cabinet
حُكومة ظِلّ	shadow cabinet
صُفوف القِيادة	leadership ranks
بَرْلمان	parliament
هَيْئة التَشْريعيّة العُلْيا	upper house
هَيْئة التَشْريعيّة الدُنْيا	lower house
مَقَرّ المَكْتَبِ السياسيّ	the political headquarters
قَصْر، قُصور	palace
بَلاط	court (royal)

مُنَظَّمة \ تَنْظيم، ـات	organisation
مُؤَسَّسة، ـات	establishment, foundation
سُلْطة	authority
السُلْطات	the authorities
سُلْطة مُؤَقَّتة	interim authority
سُلْطة مُطْلَقة	absolute power
حُكْم	rule
نِظام، أَنْظِمة	regime
رِئاسة	leadership
بِرِئاسة \ بِقِيادة \ بِزَعامة	under the leadership of (+ idafah)
سِيادة	sovereignty
وَفْد، وُفود	delegation
طاقِم، طَواقِم	team, crew
فِرقة الوِساطة، فِرَق الوِساطة	team of mediators
وَسيط ، وُسَطاء	mediator
مَبْعوث، ـون	delegate, envoy
مَنْدوب، ـون	agent, representative
مُمَثِّل، ـون	representative
مَبْعوث خاصّ	special envoy
مُفَوَّض سامٍ	high commissioner
مَسْؤول، ـون	official

كِبار المسْؤُولين	high-ranking officials
واضِعو السِياسات	policy-makers
رَئيس، رُؤَساء	president
وَزير، وُزَراء	minister
رَئيس الوُزَراء	prime minister
صاحِب المَقام	incumbent
مَنْصِب رِئاسةِ الوُزَراء	the office of prime minister
نائِب، نُوّاب	member of parliament (MP), delegate
سِياسيّ، -ون	politician
قائِد، قُوّاد \ قادة	leader
زَعيم، زُعَماء	"
مَرْجِع، مَراجِع	authority (e.g. cleric)
مُسْتَشار، -ون	consultant
مُحَلِّل، -ون	analyst
نَظير، نُظَراء	counterpart, peer
ثائِر، ثُوّار	rebel, insurgent, revolutionary
مُتَمَرِّد، -ون	rebel
مُنْشَقّ، -ون	dissident
مُنافِس، -ون	rival, competitor
خَصْم، خُصُوم	opponent
مُؤَيِّد، -ون	supporter

مُتَعاطِف، -ون	sympathiser
ناشِط \ مُنَشِّط، -ون	activist
مُسْتَوْطِن، -ون	settler
مُساعِد، -ون	aide
مُتَشائِم، -ون	pessimist
مُتَفائِل، -ون	optimist
عُضْو، أَعْضاء	member
عُضْوِيَة	membership
مَلِك، مُلوك	king
مَلِكة، -ات	queen
عاهِل، عَواهِل	monarch
وَلِي العَهْد	Crown Prince
صاحِب الجَلالة	His Majesty
سُلْطان، سَلاطين	sultan
أَمير، أُمَراء	prince
والٍ، وُلاة	governor, ruler
خادِم الحَرَمَين الشَريفَين	Guardian of the Two Shrines (i.e. Saudi king)
سَفير، سُفَراء	ambassador
الأَمين العامّ	the Secretary General
مُتَحَدِّث بِاسْم \ ناطِق بِاسْم	spokesperson
رائِد، رُوّاد	pioneer

جُمْهوريّة، ـات	republic
دَوْلة، دُوَل	state
وَطَن، أَوْطان	nation, homeland
شَعْب، شُعوب	a people
قَوْم، أَقْوام	"
بِلاد، بُلْدان	country
دَوْلة قَوْميّة	nation-state
عاصِمة، عَواصِم	capital (geographical)
ميزان القُوَى	the balance of power
نِظام عالَميّ جَديد	new world order
مُجْتَمَع مَدَنيّ	civil society
دَوْلة مارِقة	rogue state
الدُوَل العُظْمَى	the Superpowers
دُوَل الخليج	the Gulf States
الأراضي المُحْتَلّة	the Occupied Territories
الضِفّة الغَرْبيّة	the West Bank
قِطاع غَزّة	the Gaza Strip
الإحْتِلال	the Occupation
مُخَيَّم، ـات	(refugee) camp
مُسْتَوْطَنات	settlements
حُقوق الإنْسان	human rights
دَوائر سياسيّة	political circles

أَوْساط سياسيّة	political circles
مَصالِح مُرَسَّخة	entrenched interests
حَياة عامّة	public life
دُسْتور، دَساتير	constitution
وَثيقة، وَثائِق	draft bill, charter; document
لائِحة، ـات \ لَوائِح	bill, motion
مَرْسوم، مَراسيم	act, decree
سياسة، ـات	policy
مَبْدأ، مَبادِئ	principle
تَيّار، ـات	trend, current
اِتِّجاه، ـات	direction
اِخْتِلاف، ـات	difference
فَرْق، فُروق	"
فارِق، فَوارِق	difference, distinction
تَشابُه، ـات	similarity
بَرْنامِج، بَرامِج	programme
إصْلاح، ـات	reform
قَرار، ـات	decision
قَرار الأُمَم المتَّحِدة	UN resolution
ديموقراطيَة	democracy
نِظام الجَدارة	meritocracy
تَحْديث	modernisation

حَقيبة، حَقائِب	ministerial portfolio
تَوَلَّى حَقيبة	to take over the portfolio of (+ idafah)
تَعْديل وِزاريّ	cabinet reshuffle
أَوْراق اِعْتِماد	credentials
سَلام	peace
مُصالَحة	conciliation
دِبْلوماسيّة	diplomacy
عَفْو عَن	amnesty for
حَلّ	solution
حَلّ وَسَط	compromise
تَسْوية مَطالِب	settlement of demands
تَسْوية سِلْميّة	peace settlement
مُعاهَدة سلام	peace treaty/accord
عَمَليّة سلام	peace process
تَعَهُّد، ـات بِ	pledge
اِتِّفاق \ اِتِّفاقيّة، ـات	agreement
حِلْف	pact, alliance
تَقارُب	rapprochement
عُزْلة \ عَزْل	isolation
اِئْتِلاف	coalition
تَنْسيق بَين	alignment

حِوار، ـات	dialogue
شِعار، ـات	slogan, watchword
قِمّة، قِمَم	summit
مُؤْتَمَر ، ـات	conference, congress
اِجْتِماع، ـات	meeting, gathering
لِقاء، ـات	meeting
مُواجَهة	encounter
مُفاوَضات	negotiations
مُباحَثات \ مُحادَثات	talks, discussions
مُشاوَرة، ـات	consultation
مُناقَشة، ـات	discussion
مُبادَرة، ـات	initiative
خِيار، ـات	choice, option
مُقْتَرَحة، ـات	suggestion
نَصيحة، نَصائِح	advice
رَدّ فِعْل، رُدود فِعْل \ أَفْعال	reaction
إجْراءات	measures
إجْراءات اِسْتِثْنائِيّة	exceptional measures
مُسْتَجِدّات	innovations, recent measures
بذل يبذِل بَذْل جَهْداً \ جُهوداً	to exert effort
جَوْلة، ـات	round (of talks); tour

دَوْرة، ـات	round (of talks)
دَوْرة بَرْلمانيّة	parliamentary term/session
جَلْسة، ـات	session, sitting
مَرْحَلة، مَراحِل	stage, phase
تَقْدير لِ	appreciation of/for
عَلاقات ثُنائيّة	bilateral relations
عَلاقات ثُلاثِيّة	trilateral relations
عَلاقات مُتَعَدِّدة الأَطْراف	multi-lateral relations
تَطْبيع العَلاقات	the normalisation of relations
أعاد\ قطع العَلاقات الدِبْلوماسِيّة مَع	to resume/cut diplomatic relations with
ضَغْط، ضُغوط	pressure
تَوَتُّر، ـات	tension
تَرَدُّد	hesitation
تَقَدُّم	progress
دَفْعة قَويّة في الاتِّجاه الصَحيح	a strong step in the right direction
طَفْرة نَوْعيّة	quantum leap
نُقْطة تَحَوُّل	turning point
حِرْمان مِن	prevention of
تَخَلُّف	backwardness
الحالة الراهِنة	the status quo
اِسْتِقْلال	independence

وَحْدة	unity
ثَوْرة، ـات	revolution
اِنْقِلاب، ـات	revolt, coup
تَغْيير النِظام	regime change
اِنْتِفاضة	uprising
اِسْتِنْكار	disapproval, horror
صِمام الأمان	safety valve
مُنافَسات طائِفِيّة	sectarian rivalries
واجَه	to encounter, face
ثار يَثور ثَوْرة	to revolt
قاوَم	to resist
عارَض	to oppose
رفض يرفُض رَفْض	to reject, veto
صارَع \ نازَع \ قاتَل	to fight
ناضَل \ كافَح	to struggle
منع يمنَع مَنْع ه من \ عن	to prevent s.t./s.o. from
بذر يبذُر بُذورَ الفِتْنة والشِقاق	to sow the seeds of conflict
أثار جَدَلاً	to cause controversy
نافَس عَلَى	to contend, compete for
اِنْهار يَنْهار اِنْهيار	to fall, collapse
أسْقَط النِظام	to topple the regime

خلع يخلَع خلْع الحاكِم	to oust the ruler
سَلَّم السُلْطة	to hand over power/authority
نقل ينقُل نَقْل السُلْطة إلَى	to transfer power to
أَحَلَّ مَحَلَّهُ	to take the place of
أعاد الديموقراطيّة	to reinstate democracy
تَوَلَّى	to take over, control
إسْتَوْلَى عَلَى	to overwhelm, overcome
طغَى يَطْغَى طغْى \ طُغْيان عَلَى	to seize, overcome, terrorise
سَيْطَر عَلَى	to dominate, control, seize
قمع يقَمَع قَمْع	to suppress, repress
تَحَرَّش بِ	to harrass
عَلَّق	to suspend
أزال يُزيل إزالة	to remove, sideline, get rid of
هَمَّش	to marginalise
ألْغَى يُلْغي إلْغاء	to abolish
أقال يُقيل إقالة	to dismiss
عزل يعزِل عَزْل	to remove
حلّ يحُلّ حَلّ نَفْسَه	to dissolve itself
فَكَّك	to disband (v.t.)
إعْتَزَل مِن	to withdraw from
إنْشَقّ عَن	to break away, secede, split off from

تَفَكَّك	to disintegrate, break up
وضع يَضِع وَضْع حَدّاً لِ	to put an end to
أَنْهَى	to end (v.t.)
اِنْتَهَى	to end (v.i.)
أَفْسَح المَجال أَمامَ	to clear the way for
اِنْتَمَى إلَى	to belong to
أَوْشَك عَلَى	to be on the point of
عقد يعقِد عَقْد	to convene, hold (meeting)
اِنْعَقَد	to be convened
أَجْرَى يُجْري إِجْراء	to hold (talks)
نَسَّق	to arrange
اِسْتَأْنَف	to resume
جَدَّد	to renew
حضر يحضُر حُضور	to attend, be present
اِسْتَغْرَق	to last
اِسْتَمَرَّ	to continue
أَجَّل يُؤَجِّل تَأْجيل	to postpone
أَخَّر يُؤَخِّر تَأْخير	to delay
تَأَخَّر	to be delayed
أَطال	to prolong
اِسْتَقْبَل	to receive (visitor)
اِلْتَقَى بِ	to meet with

قام يقوم قِيام بِرِحْلة	to take/make a trip
قام بِزيارة رَسْميّة	to pay a state/official visit
بِدَعْوة مِن	at the invitation of
سافَر	to travel
وصل يَصِل وُصول إلَى	to arrive in
بلغ يبلُغ بُلوغ	to reach
غادَر	to depart
عاد يعود عَوْدة	to return
رجع يرجِع رُجوع	"
تَوَجَّه إلَى	to head for
في طَريق عَوْدتِهِ مِن	on his way back from
في خِتام زيارتِهِ إلَى	at the end of his visit to
اِخْتَتَم زيارةً	to conclude a visit
رافَق \ اِصْطَحَب	to accompany
أرْسَل \ بعث يبعَث بَعْث	to send
قَدَّم	to present, offer
سَلَّم	to hand over
منح يمنَح مَنْح	to award, grant, confer
تَسَلَّم	to obtain, receive
حصل يحصُل حُصول عَلَى	to get hold of, obtain
تَلَقَّى	to receive, obtain, take
اِتَّفَق عَلَى	to agree on

وَقَّع	to sign
قَرَّر	to decide, resolve
عزم يعزِم عَزْم عَلَى	to decide on, determine
حسم يحسِم حَسْم	to settle, decide
سَوَّى يُسَوِّي تَسْوية	to settle
تَبَنَّى قَرارًا	to adopt a resolution
أَبْقَى خياراتِهِ مَفْتوحة	to keep one's options open
أَسْقَط خيارًا	to rule out an option
شَكَّل يُشَكِّل تَشْكيل	to form, shape
أقام	to set up, erect, hold
أَسَّس يُؤَسِّس تَأْسيس	to found, establish
ثَبَّت	to stabilise, secure
رَسَّخ	to entrench
عَزَّز	to strengthen
دعم يدعَم دَعْم	to support
أَيَّد يُؤَيِّد تَأْييد	"
سانَد	to back
شَجَّع ه عَلَى	to encourage s.o. to do s.t.
تَواطَأ مع	to collude with
مال يميل مَيْل إلَى	to lean towards, favour
دعا يَدْعو دَعْوة ه إلَى	to call on s.o. to
طَوَّر	to develop (v.t.)

تَطَوَّر	to develop (v.i.)
نَمَّى	to promote, develop (v.t.)
تَنَمَّى	to grow, develop (v.i.)
وَسَّع	to expand (v.t.)
تَوَسَّع	to expand (v.i.)
حَوَّل \ غَيَّر	to change, transform (v.t.)
تَحَوَّل \ تَغَيَّر	to change (v.i.)
حَسَّن	to improve (v.t.)
تَحَسَّن	to improve (v.i.)
قام يَقوم قيام بِ	to undertake
أدار يُدير إدارة	to direct, administer
اِتَّخَذ	to adopt (e.g. measures)
اِعْتَنَق	to embrace (doctrine; person)
وَجَّه ه إلَى	to orientate s.t. towards
أشْرَف عَلَى	to supervise, oversee, watch over
راقَب	to monitor, censor
دَقَّق \ مَحَّص	to scrutinise
أصْبَح أمْراً واقِعاً	to become a reality
طرأ يطرَأ طَرْءاً\طُروء عَلَى	to befall, happen to s.o.
جرى يجري جَرْي	to occur, happen
حدث يحدُث حَدَث	"
وقع يَقَع وُقوع	"

بدا يَبْدو	to seem
ظهر يظهَر ظُهور	to emerge, appear, seem
عاد إلَى الظُهور	to reappear, re-emerge
حَقَّق	to fulfil, realise
نَفَّذ	to implement, carry out
مارَس	to practise
اِتَّخَذ خَطَوات	to take steps
كان مَضْرِب المَثَل	to be exemplary/a byword
فرض يفرُض فَرْض عُقوبات	to impose sanctions
رفع يرفع رَفْع عُقوبات	to lift sanctions
قاطَع	to boycott
طلب يطلُب طَلَب اللُجوء السياسيّ	to seek political asylum
ربط يربُط رَبْط بَين	to link, unite
اِرْتَبَط بِ	to be linked to
تَعَلَّق بِ	to be related to
راوَح بَين	to fluctuate between
ضغط يضغط ضَغْط عَلَى	to put pressure on
خَفَّف مِن	to mitigate, ease (v.t.)
تَضاءَل	to fade, dwindle, diminish
خطِف يخطَف خَطْف الأَضْواء	to snatch the limelight

عانَى مِن	to suffer from
أُصِيب يُصاب إصابة بِ	to be afflicted by (Arabic passive)

3. ELECTIONS

اِنْتِخاب، ـات	election
اِنْتِخابات فَرْعيّة	by-elections
اِنْتِخابات عامّة	general elections
اِنْتِخابات رِئاسيّة	presidential elections
اِنْتِخابات فيدِراليّة	federal elections
اِنْتِخابات مَحَلّيّة	local elections
اِنْتِخابات التَجْديد النِصْفيّ	mid-term elections
دَوْرة ثانية لِلْاِنْتِخابات	run-off election
اِنْتِخابات مُبكّرة	early elections
اِنْتِخابات حُرّة ونَزيهة	free and fair elections
نِظام الحِزْبِ الواحِد	one-party system
نِظام الأَحْزابِ المُتَعَدِّدة	multi-party system
تَمْثيل نِسْبيّ	proportional representation
نِظام أَكْثَريّ	majority system
عَمَليّة اِنْتِخابيّة	electoral process
لَجْنة اِنْتِخابيّة	electoral commission
رَقابة اِنْتِخابيّة	election monitoring
اِسْتِفْتاء	referendum
اِسْتِطْلاع رَأي	opinion poll
الرَأي العامّ	public opinion

اِقْتِراع، ـات	ballot
اِقْتِراع سِرّيّ	secret ballot
صُنْدوق اِقْتِراع	ballot box
مَرْكَز اِقْتِراع	polling station
تَصْويت عَلَى الثِقة	vote of confidence
تَصْويت بِسَحْب الثِقة	vote of no-confidence
حَمْلة، حَمَلات	campaign
بَيان اِنْتِخابيّ	election manifesto
مُرَشَّح، ـون	candidate
مُرَشَّح مُسْتقِلّ	independent candidate
شَخْصيّة، ـات	personality
صورة، صُوَر	image
شُهْرة	reputation
اِشْتِهار	notoriety
شَعْبيّة	popularity
تَراجُع في الشَعْبيّة	decline in popularity
إلْغاء التَرْشيح	de-selection
لائِحة حِزْبيّة	party list
وَلاء لِ	loyalty to
غَيْر الناخِبين	non-voters
مُسَجَّلون في قَوائِمِ الإقْتِراع	registered voters

الناخِبون	the electorate
اِنْتِخابيّ	electoral
لائحة اِنْتِخابيّة	electoral roll
سِجِلّ الناخِبين	register of electors
دائِرة اِنْتِخابيّة	constituency
مَقْعد، مَقاعِد	seat
صَوْت أَصْوات	vote
اِنْتِصار، ـات	victory
وِلاية ثانية	second term
أَغْلَبيّة مُطْلَقة	absolute majority
بَرْلمان مُعَلَّق	hung parliament
تَزْوير الاِنْتِخابات	election-rigging
تَزْوير الدَوائِر	gerrymandering
شَفَافيّة	transparency
عَتَبة، عَتَب \ أَعْتاب	threshold
نِسْبة المُشارَكة	turnout
فَرْز الأَصْوات	vote count
إعادة فَرْزِ الأَصْوات	re-count
الحِزْب الأَكْثَر اِتّساعاً	the most widespread party
الحِزْب الأَسْرَع نُمُواً	the fastest-growing party
دِعاية	propaganda
أَجْرَى اِنْتِخابات	to hold elections

أَجَّل اِنْتِخابات	to delay elections
أَلْغَى اِنْتِخابات	to cancel elections
صَوَّت	to vote
اِنْتَخَب	to elect
أَعاد الاِنْتِخاب	to re-elect
أَحْجَم عَن	to abstain from
فاز يفوز فَوْز في	to gain, win (votes) in
أَحْرَز اِنْتِصاراً ساحِقاً	to win a landslide victory
أَحْرَز أَغْلَبِيّة ساحِقة	to secure an overwhelming majority
أخذ يأخُذ أَخْذ أَعِنَّة الحُكومة	to take up the reins of government
وصل يَصِل وُصول إلى السُلْطة	to come to power
رَشَّح	to nominate
نَصَّب	to appoint

4. MILITARY

المُؤَسَّسة الْعَسْكَرِيّة	the military
العَسْكَرِيّون	"
جَيْش، جُيوش	army
القُوّات المُسَلَّحة	the armed forces
قُوّة مُتَعَدِّدة الجِنْسِيّات	multinational force
القُوّات	the troops
رُكُن، أَرْكان	military staff
جُنْدِيّ، جُنود	soldier
مَدَنِيّ، -ون	civilian
المُشاة	the infantry (Arabic pl.)
بَحّار، -ون \ بَحّارة	sailor
جُنْدِيّ مُشاةِ البَحْريّة	marine
طَيّار، -ون	airman, pilot
مِظَلّيّ، -ون	paratrooper
قانِص، قُنّاص	sniper
بَطَل، أَبْطال	hero
مُنْشِقّ، -ون	defector
شارِد، شَوارِد \ شُرُد	deserter
أَسير حَرْب، أَسْرَى حَرْب	POW (prisoner of war)
تَبادُل الأَسْرَى	prisoner exchange

مُجْرِم حَرْب، مُجْرِمو حَرْب	war criminal
حَليف، حُلَفاء	ally, confederate
لِواء، أَلْوية	General; flag
رَئيس الأَرْكان	Chief of Staff
رُتْبة، رُتَب	rank, grade
قُوّة جَوِّيّة	air force
قُوّات بَرِّيّة	ground forces
قُوّات اِحْتِياطِيّة	reserves
قُوّة خاصّة	commando, special troop
قُوّة خَفيفة	light/mobile task force
قِطَعات قِتالِيّة	combat troops
قُوّات حِفْظِ السَلام	peacekeeping forces
قُوّات تَحالُف	coalition forces
قُوّة دِفاعِيّة	defence force
قُوّة هُجُومِيّة ضارِبة	strike force
قُوّة رَدْع	deterrent force
فَصيلة، فَصائِل	cell, squad
فَصيلة الإعْدام	execution squad, firing squad
دَوْريّة، ـات	patrol
وَحْدة، وَحَدات	(military) unit
سِرْب، أَسْراب	squadron
كَتيبة، كَتائِب	battalion

ميليشيا، ميليشيات	militia
سِلاح، أَسْلِحة	weapon
أَسْلِحة خَفيفة \ صَغيرة	small arms
ذَخيرة	ammunition
مِظَلَّة، ـات	parachute
تَرْسانة، ـات	arsenal
أَسْلِحة نَوَويّة	nuclear weapons
رَدْع نَوَويّ	nuclear deterrent
أَسْلِحة ذَكِيّة	precision weapons
سِباق تَسَلُّح	arms race
أَسْلِحة الدَمارِ الشامِل	WMD (weapons of mass destruction)
صاروخ، صَواريخ	missile, rocket
صاروخ مُضادّ لِلطائِرات	anti-aircraft missile
صاروخ تَمْويهيّ	decoy missile
صاروخ طَوّاف	cruise missile
صاروخ سَطْح - جَوّ	surface-to-air missile
صاروخ بَعيد \ قَصير المَدَى	long-/short-range missile
قَذيفة عابِرة لِلقارّات	intercontinental ballistic missile
قاذِفة الصَواريخ	rocket/missile launcher
نَسيفة، نَسائِف	torpedo
قُنْبُلة، قَنابِل	bomb

أَداة تَفْجير	explosive device
مُتَفَجِّرات	explosives
قُنْبُلة يَدَوِيّة	hand grenade
قُنْبُلة نَوَوِيّة	nuclear bomb
قُنْبُلة ذَرِّيّة	atomic bomb
قُنْبُلة عُنْقودِيّة	cluster bomb
قُنْبُلة حارِقة	incendiary bomb
قَذيفة هاوُن، قَذائِف هاوُن	mortar bomb
لَغَم \ لُغْم، أَلْغام	mine
رَصاصة، ـات \ رَصاص	bullet
مِدْفَع، مَدافِع	gun
مُسَدَّس، ـات	revolver
مِدْفَع رَشّاش	machine gun
رَشّاش قَصير	sub-machine gun
بُنْدُقِيّة آلِيّة	automatic rifle
سِلاح قَذّافيّ	ballistic weapon
قِطْعة مِدْفَعِيّة	(piece of) artillery
قَصْف مِدْفَعيّ	artillery fire
قَصْف صاروخيّ	rocket fire
شَظايا	shrapnel (Arabic pl.)
إشْعاع	radiation
انْفِجار \ تَفْجير، ـات	explosion

عَصْف	blast
قَصْف	bombardment, shelling
قَصْف دَقيق \ ذَكيّ	precision bombing
ضَرْبة وِقائيّة	preemptive strike
اِسْتِخْدام القُوّة	use of force
غِطاء جَوّيّ	air cover
دِفاعات جَوّيّة	air defences
مِنْطَقة حَظْر جَوّيّ	no-fly zone
مِنْطَقة مَنْزوعة السِلاح	demilitarised zone
مِنْطَقة القِتال	combat zone
مِنْطَقة خالية مِن الأَسْلِحة النَوَويّة	nuclear-free zone
ناقِلة جُنود مُدَرَّعة	armoured personnel carrier
دَبَّابة، ـات	tank
جَرّافة، ـات	bulldozer
طائِرة مِرْوَحيّة \ هَليكوبْتَر	helicopter
غَوّاصة مُضادّة لِلطائِرات	anti-aircraft submarine
حامِلة طائِرات	aircraft carrier
طائِرة مُقاتِلة	fighter aircraft
طائِرة مِنْ دونَ طَيّار	drone
مُدَمِّرة، ـات	destroyer
سَفينة حَرْبيّة، سُفُن حَرْبيّة	warship
بارِجة، بَوارِج	frigate

زَوْرَق حَرْبيّ، زَوارِق حَرْبيّة	gunboat
نَسّافة، ـات	torpedo boat
أُسْطول، أَساطيل	fleet
قَاعِدة عَسْكَريّة، قَواعِد عَسْكَريّة	military base
مَقَرّ، مَقارّ	headquarters (HQ)
مَوْقِع اسْتِراتيجيّ، مَواقِع اسْتِراتيجيّة	strategic point
اِنْتِشار الأَسْلِحة النَوَويّة	nuclear proliferation
عَدَم الإنْتِشار النَوَويّ	nuclear non-proliferation
جِهاز طَرْد مَرْكَزيّ	centrifugal system
تَخْصيب اليورانيوم	enrichment of uranium
حَرْب، حُروب	war (Arabic fem.)
حَرْب أَهْليّة	civil war
حَرْب عِصابات	guerilla warfare
حَرْب بِالوَكالة	proxy war
حَرْب عادِلة	just war
جَريمة حَرْب، جَرائِم حَرْب	war crime
في حالةِ الحَرْب	at war
مَسْرَح الحَرْب	theatre of war
ميدان العَمَليّات	field of operations
مُناوَرة، ـات	manoeuvre
اِسْتِطْلاع	reconnaissance

إِسْتِعْراض \ عَرْض	parade
مَعْرَكة، مَعارِك	battle
خَطَر، أَخْطار \ مَخاطِر	danger
أَمْن	safety
دَرْع بَشَرِيّ، دُروع بَشَرِيّة	human shield
وَقْف إطْلاقِ النار	ceasefire
حَلّ النِزاعات	conflict resolution
تَجْريد مِن السِلاح	disarmament; demilitarisation
مَجْزَرة، مَجازِر	massacre
إبادة جَماعِيّة	genocide
تَطْهير عِرْقِيّ	ethnic cleansing
مَصْرَع، مَصارِع	death; battleground
تَدَخُّل عَسْكَرِيّ	military intervention
جِنازة، ـات \ جَنائِز	funeral (procession)
مُباغَتة، ـات	surprise attack
غارة، ـات	raid
هُجوم بَرّيّ	ground offensive, land attack
هُجوم بَرْمائِيّ	amphibious attack
هُجوم إرْهابِيّ	terrorist attack
هُجوم مُسَلَّح عَلَى	armed attack on
هُجوم مُضادّ	counter attack
كَمين	ambush

تَكْتيكات	tactics
اِعْتِداءات عَلَى	aggressions against
رَدّ اِنْتِقاميّ عَلى	revenge for
عَلَى مَتْن	on board (a ship/aircraft) (+ idafah)
في وَضْع اِسْتِعْداد لِ	in a state of readiness for
مُنْتَشِر	deployed
عُدْوانيّ \ عَدائيّ	hostile
اِنْعِكاسات \ عَواقِب	repercussions
حشد يحشُد حَشْد	to mobilise, call up to accumulate
حشَّد	to amass (especially troops)
جنَّد	to draft, conscript, mobilise
اِسْتَدْعَى	to call up
عَزَّز القُوّات	to reinforce the troops
نشر ينشُر نَشْر	to deploy
تَفَقَّد	to inspect
فَجَّر	to explode (v.t.)
تَفَجَّر	to explode (v.i.)
دَمَّر \ هَدَّم	to destroy
أَباد \ أَفْنَى	to annihilate
قضَى يقضي قَضاء عَلَى تَمَرُّد	to put down a revolt

أَوْدَى بِحَياة	to claim the life/lives of (+ idafah)
اُسْتُشْهِد	to be martyred (Arabic passive)
أُصيبَ بِجُروح خَطيرة \ طَفيفة	to suffer serious/minor injuries (Arabic passive)
هجم يهجُم هُجوم عَلَى	to attack
غزا يَغْزو غَزْو	to attack, invade, raid
أَعْلَن الحَرْب	to declare war
شنّ يشُنّ شَنّ هُجوماً \ حَمْلةً	to launch an attack/campaign
أطْلَق	to launch (missile, torpedo, etc.)
اِقْتَحَم	to storm
تَسَلَّل إلَى	to infiltrate
تَوَغَّل في	to advance further, to penetrate deeply into
حاصَر	to besiege, surround
فتح يفتَح فَتْح النار	to open fire
أطْلَق النار	"
تَبادَل إطْلاق النار	to exchange fire
دافَع عَن	to defend
حمى يحمي حِماية ه مِن	to protect s.t. against
اِنْسَحَب	to withdraw (v.i.)
جلا يجلو جَلاء عَن	to evacuate, pull out of
أَجْلَى	to evacuate (v.t.)

اِسْتَسْلَم	to surrender
أَطْلَق	to free
أَطْلَق سَراحَهُ	to set s.o. free
اِسْتَأْنَف القِتال	to resume fighting
قاوَم	to resist
خَطَّط	to plan
تَآمَر	to plot
اِسْتَهْدَف تَحْديداً	to target specifically
نصب ينصُب نَصْب حَواجِز عَلَى الطُرُق	to erect road blocks
فرض يفرُض فَرْض حِصاراً عَلَى	to impose a cordon/ blockade on
اِنْدَلَع	to break out (war)
اِحْتَلّ	to occupy
اِخْتَرَق الحُدود	to cross the border(s)
قَدَّر حَجْمَ القُوّات بِ	to estimate the strength of forces at
اِسْتَخْلَص المعْلومات	to debrief

5. ECONOMICS

الإقْتِصاد العالَميّ	the global economy
الإحْتِياطيّ الإتِّحاديّ	the Federal Reserve
السوق المُشْتَرَكة	the Common Market
البَنْك الدُوَليّ	the World Bank
صُنْدوق النَقْدِ الدُوَليّ	IMF (International Monetary Fund)
البَنْك المَرْكَزيّ الأوروبيّ	ECB (European Central Bank)
صُنْدوق الاسْتِقْرار الماليّ الأورُوبّيّ	EFSF (European Financial Stability Facility)
الناتِج المَحَلّيّ الإجْماليّ	GDP (Gross Domestic Product)
مِنْطَقة اليورو	the Euro zone
إصْلاح اقْتِصاديّ	economic reform
أزْمة ماليّة	financial crisis
اِنْهِيار ماليّ	financial meltdown
رُكود	recession
تَدَهْوُر	decline, slump
اِنْتِعاش اقْتِصاديّ	economic recovery
إنْقاذ	bailout
حُزْمة إنْقاذ	rescue package
مُعاهَدة الاسْتِقْرار	stability pact
إجْراءات تَقَشُّفِيَة	austerity measures

إنْفاق عامّ	public spending
خَفْض إنْفاق	spending cut(s)
تَخْفيضات	cutbacks
سوق سَوْداء	black market
سوق حُرّة	free market
سوق النَقْد \ البورصة	the Stock Exchange
أسْواق الصَرْف	exchange markets
أسْواق العُمْلات الأجْنَبِيّة	foreign currency markets
اِحْتياطات النَقْد الأجْنَبِيّ	foreign currency reserves
تَكامُل اِقْتِصاديّ	economic integration
عُقوبات اِقْتِصاديّة	economic sanctions
مُقاطَعة	boycott
لَدَى إغْلاق التَداوُل	at the close of trade
عُمْلة صَعْبة	hard currency
عُمْلة سَهْلة	soft currency
رَأْس مال، رُؤوس أموال	capital
رَأْسْمال، رَساميل	"
دَخْل	income
قُوّة الشِراء	purchasing power
اِحْتِكار، ـات	monopoly; cartel
قُوّات السُوق	market forces
تَنافُس	competition

قُدْرة تَنافُسِيّة	competitiveness
سِعْر الصَرْف	exchange rate
سِعْر الفائِدة	interest rate
نقْطة مِئوية	percentage point
فائِدة مُيَسَّرة	preferential rate of interest
كُلْفة الإقْتِراض	cost of borrowing
سِعْر البَيْع	retail price
سِعْر اليورو مُقابِلَ الدولار	the price of the euro against the dollar
مُسْتَوى مُرْتَفَع غَيْر مَسْبوق	a new high
سَهْم، أَسْهُم	share
سَنَد، ـات	bond
سَنَد خُرْدة	junk bond
مُشْتَقّات	derivatives
ضَريبة، ضَرائِب	tax
ضَريبة الدَخْل	income tax
ضَريبة القيمة المُضافة	VAT (value added tax)
ضَريبة الأرْباح الرَأسْماليّة	CGT (capital gains tax)
ضَريبة التَرِكات	inheritance tax
ضَريبة عَقاريّة	property tax
إعْفاء مِن الضَرائِب	tax exemption
تَخْفيضات ضَريبيّة	tax cuts
بِالمائة \ بِالمِئة	per cent

اِسْتِثْمار، ـات	investment
وَديعة، وَدائع	deposit
أَصْل، أُصول	asset
عائِد، ـات	dividend, return
إيراد، ـات	revenue, profit
حَصيلة، حَصائِل	income, yield
مَبْلَغ، مَبالِغ	amount
رِبْح، أَرْباح	profit
مُرْبِح	profitable
مُفْلِس	bankrupt
تَكاليف	costs
نَفَقات	expenses
إجْماليّ	total, gross
صافٍ \ الصافي	net
بَعْد اِسْتِبْعاد أَثَرِ التَضَخُّم	in real terms
مُساندة الأسْعار مِن طَرْفِ الدَوْلة	price control
اِسْتِقْرار الأسْعار	price stability
القَرْية الكَوْنيّة	the global village
عَوْلَمة	globalisation
غَسيل الأمْوال	money laundering
تَضَخُّم	inflation
مُعَدَّل التَضَخُّم	rate of inflation

تَخْفيض القيمة	devaluation
مُضارَبة	speculation
تَكَهُّن، ‐ات	forecasting
عَدَم الإسْتِقْرار	instability
تَذَبْذُب	fluctuation
إفْلاس	bankruptcy
مُسْتَوَى المَعيشة	standard of living
قُوّة الشِراء	purchasing power
دَيْن، دُيُون	debt
دَيْن عامّ	public debt
دَيْن مُسْتَحَقّ	outstanding debt
أزْمة الدُيون	debt crisis
قَرْض، قُرُوض	loan
فَتْرة سَماح	grace period
عَجْز في ميزانيّة الدَوْلة	budget deficit
عَجْز تِجاريّ	trade deficit
قيمة العَجْز	the amount of the deficit
فائِض، فَوائِض	surplus
سُيولة	liquidity
إقْتِصاد الحَجْم	economy of scale
العام الماليّ \ السَّنة الماليّة	the financial year
رَقْم قِياسيّ	record figure

إحْصائيّات	statistics
مُؤَشِّر، ـات	index, indicator
سِلْعة، سِلَع	commodity
مُعَدَّل اِسْتِهْلاك	the average consumption of (+ idafah)
وَزير الماليّة	finance minister
مُمَوِّل، ـون	financier
اِقْتِصاديّ، ـون	economist
مُعامِل، ـون	trader, dealer
سِمْسار، سَماسِرة	broker
مُضارِب، ـون	speculator
مُساهِم، ـون	shareholder
مُسْتَثْمِر، ـون	investor
مُعير، ـون	lender
مُسْتَعير، ـون	borrower
مُسْتَهْلِك، ـون	consumer
أصْحاب الثَرَوات الطائِلة	the super-rich
شَريك تِجاريّ، شُرَكاء تِجاريّون	trade partner
نَفَّذ عُقوبات اِقْتِصاديّة	to apply economic sanctions
مَوَّل	to finance
شَغَّل رَأْسْمالاً	to invest capital
أنْفَق	to spend

ضارَب	to speculate
أضاع	to squander
كَلَّف	to cost
كَثَّف	to consolidate
ازْدَهَر	to blossom, flourish
أفْلَح	to prosper, thrive
خَفَّض العَجْز في الميزانيّة	to reduce the budget deficit
رفع يرفَع رَفْع \ خَفَّض أسْعار الفائِدة	to raise/cut interest rates
رفع يرفَع رَفْع \ خَفَّض الضَرائِب	to raise/lower taxes
دخل يدخُل دُخول حَيِّزَ التَنْفيذ	to come into effect
نَشَّط الاقْتِصاد	to stimulate the economy
سدّ يسُدّ سَدّ \ سَداد دَيْناً	to repay a debt
أخْفَق في سَداد دُيون	to default
أعاد جَدْوَل دَيْن	to reschedule a debt
أعْفَى ه مِن دَيْن	to cancel, write off a debt
جَمَّد دَيْناً	to freeze a debt
اسْتَحَقّ	to become payable
أفْلَس	to become bankrupt
ربط يربُط رَبْط الْعُمْلة بِالدّولار	to tie the currency to the dollar

6. TRADE & INDUSTRY

تِجارة	trade
صِناعة	industry
مُنَظَّمة التِجارةِ العالَميّة	WTO (World Trade Organization)
مَجْموعة الثَّماني	G8 (Group of 8 Industrialised Countries)
مَجْموعة العِشْرين	G20 (Group of 20 Industrialised Countries)
أُوبَك	OPEC
مُنَظَّمة الدُوَلِ المُصَدِّرة للنَفْط	Organization of the Petroleum Exporting Countries
الدُوَل المُنْتِجة للنَفْط غَيْر الأعْضاء في أُوبَك	non-OPEC
دُوَل نامية	developing countries
دُوَل مُتَقَدِّمة	developed countries
قِطاع عامَ	public sector
قِطاع خاصّ	private sector
صادِرات	exports
وارِدات	imports
حَجْم التِجارة	volume of trade
تَبادُل تِجاريّ	trade exchange
حَظْر تِجاريّ	trade embargo

مَجْموعة، ـات	conglomerate
مُساهَمة، ـات	corporation
اِمْتياز، ـات	concession, licence
شَركة ذات مَسْؤوليّة مَحْدودة	LLC (limited liability company)
شَركة المُساهَمة	JSC (joint-stock company)
شَراكة، ـات	partnership
اِنْدِماج، ـات	merger
تَقْرير سَنَويّ	annual report
هَيْكَل، هَياكِل	structure
مَصْنَع، مَصانِع	factory
مُسْتَوْدَع، ـات	warehouse
مِصْفاة، مَصافٍ	refinery
عَقار، ـات	real estate
العَرْض والطَلَب	supply and demand
بِئْر نَفْطيّة، آبار نَفْطيّة	oil well (Arabic fem.)
نَفْط خام	crude oil
إنْتاج النَفْط	oil production
بِرْميل، بَراميل	barrel
وَقُود	fuel (petrol/gas for cars)
مَوادّ خام \ خامات	raw materials
مَوادّ غِذائيّة	foodstuffs

سِلَع اِسْتِهْلاكيّة	consumer goods
ثَقافة اِسْتِهْلاكيّة	consumer culture
مَوارِد طَبيعيّة	natural resources
مَعْدَن، مَعادِن	mineral
مَعادِن ثَمينة	precious metals
مَنْجَم، مَناجِم	mine
مُدير، -ون \ مُدَراء	director, head
مُدير عامّ	Director General
مَجْلِس الإدارة	board of directors
رَجُل أَعْمال، رِجال أَعْمال	businessman
العَمالة \ القُوَى العامِلة	the workforce
عَمَل فَريقيّ	teamwork
مُوَظَّف، -ون	employee, functionary
عامِل، عُمّال	worker
زَبون، زَبائِن	customer, client
مُسْتَهْلِك، -ون	consumer
عاطِل، -ون	unemployed person
وَظيفة، وَظائِف	job
زِيادة الأُجور	wage increase
أَدْنَى مُسْتَوَى لِلأُجور	minimum wage
دَخْل مُنْخَفَض	low income
بَطالة	unemployment

اِسْتِقالة	retirement, resignation
راتِب تَقاعُديّ	pension
إضْراب	strike
نِقابة، ‑ات	trade union
بُنْية تَحْتيّة	infrastructure
سِعْر التَشْغيل	running cost
اِقْتِصاد الحَجْم	economy of scale
إجْرائيّ	operational
دَعْم حُكوميّ	government subsidy
عَقْد، عُقود	contract
صَفْقة، صَفَقات	deal
فَساد	corruption
رَشْوة	bribery
المَسؤوليّة الاِجْتِماعيّة للشَرِكات	corporate social responsibility
خَسارة، خَسائِر	loss
ضَرَر، أَضْرار	damage
تَأْمين، ‑ات	insurance
قَيْد، قُيود	restriction
مُرونة	flexibility
مَحَطّة تَوْليدِ الكَهْرَباء	power station
مَحَطّة الطاقةِ النَوَويّة	nuclear power station

طاقة	energy
حَمْلة التَسْويق	marketing campaign
مَعْرِض تِجاريّ	trade fair
مَوْقِع شَبَكة الإِنْتَرْنَت، مَواقِع شَبَكة الإِنْتَرْنَت	website
مَعْلوماتِيّة	IT (information technology)
صَدَّر	to export
اِسْتَوْرَد \ وَرَّد	to import
وَزَّع	to distribute
زَوَّد	to supply
اِسْتَقال	to retire, resign
وَظَّف \ شَغَّل	to employ
طرد يطرُد طَرْد مِن العَمَل	to dismiss (from job)
أدار يُدير إدارة	to direct
زاد يزيد زِيادة	to increase (v.t.)
اِزْداد	to increase (v.i.)
زاد يزيد زِيادة عَن	to exceed
عَوَّض عَن	to compensate for
خَصَّص	to privatise
أمَّم	to nationalise
صَفَّى	to liquidate
أمَّن	to insure

رفع يرفَع رَفْع القُيودَ   to deregulate (lit. to lift
الحُكوميّة   government restrictions)

رَعَى يرعَى رَعْي   to sponsor

تَعامَل مَع   to do business with

7. LAW & ORDER

النِظام القَضائيّ	the judicial system
قانون، قَوانين	law
لائِحة، لَوائِح	bill
بَنْد، بُنود	article (of law)
الشَريعة	Islamic Law (Shariʿa)
مَحْكَمة، مَحاكِم	court
مَحْكَمة العَدْل الدُوَليّة	the International Court of Justice
المَحْكَمة الجِنائيّة الدُوَليّة	ICC (the International Criminal Court)
المَحْكَمة الدُوَليّة لِحُقوق الإنْسان	the International Court of Human Rights
مَحْكَمة عُلْيا	high court, supreme court
الحَرَس الوَطَنيّ	the national guard
قُوّات الأمْن	the security forces
الشُرْطة العَسْكَريّة	the military police
المُخابَرات	the intelligence service
سُلْطة قَضائيّة	judicial power, judiciary
سُلْطة تَشْريعيّة	legislative power
المُدَّعي العامّ	the attorney-general, public prosecutor

قاضٍ، قُضاة	judge
مُحلَّف، -ون	juror
هَيْئة المُحَلَّفين	jury
رَئيس النيابة	chief prosecutor
مُحامٍ، -ون	lawyer
مُدَّعٍ، -ون	plaintiff
مُدَّعٍ عليه، مُدَّعٍ عليهم	defendant
مُشْتَبَه بِهِ، مُشْتَبَه بِهم	suspect
شاهِد، شُهود	witness
شاهِد عِيان، شُهود عِيان	eyewitness
مُفَتِّش، -ون	inspector
مُحَقِّق، -ون	detective, investigator
شُرْطيّ، -ون	policeman
ضَحِيّة، ضَحايا	victim
جَريح، جَرْحَى	wounded, injured (person)
قَتيل، قَتْلَى	dead (person)
مُحْتَجّ، -ون	protester
مُتَظاهِر، -ون	demonstrator
مُشاغِب، -ون	rioter
قاتِل، قُتّال	murderer, killer
مُهَرِّب، -ون	smuggler
جاسوس، جَواسيس	spy

جاسوس مُزْدَوَج	double agent
سَجين سياسيّ، سُجَناء سياسيّون	political prisoner
أَسير، أَسْرَى	captive, prisoner
مُحْتَجَز، ـون	detainee
مُجْرِم، ـون	criminal
ذُو سَوابِق	s.o. with a (criminal) record
بَلْطَجيّ، بَلْطَجيّة	thug
مُسَلَّح، ـون	gunman
إِرْهابيّ، ـون	terrorist
مُنَفِّذ عَمَليّة اِنْتِحاريّة	suicide bomber
شَهيد، شُهَداء	martyr
رَهينة، رَهائِن	hostage
عَدُو، أَعْداء	enemy
عَدُو قَوْميّ رَقْم ١	public enemy number one
عِصابة، ـات	gang
شَبَكة، ـات	network
إِجْراءات أَمْنيّة	security measures
عَمَليّات مُكافِحة الإِرْهاب	counter-terrorist operations
حُرّيّات مَدَنيّة	civil liberties
مُراقَبة	surveillance
نُقْطة تَفْتيش، نِقاط تَفْتيش	check-point

تُهْمة، تُهَم	accusation
اِدِّعاء، ـات	allegation
قَضية، قَضايا	lawsuit
عُقوبة، ـات	punishment
اللا تَسامُح	zero tolerance
سِجْن، سُجون	prison
حَبْس اِنْفِرادِيّ	solitary confinement
كَفالة	bail
حَظْر	ban
غَرامة، ـات	fine
تَعْويض، ـات	compensation, damages
تَحْذير، ـات	warning
دَليل، أَدِلّة	evidence
مُكافَأة	reward
حَصانة	immunity
مُحاكَمة	trial
بِتُهَم	on charges of (+ idafah)
مَحْكوم بِ	sentenced to
مُدان بِ	convicted of
اِسْتِجابةً لِ	in response to
جَريمة، جَرائِم	crime, offence
جِناية، ـات	crime, felony

جَرائِم ضِدّ الإنْسانيّة	crimes against humanity
اِنْتِهاك، ـات	abuse, violation
قَسْوة	abuse, cruelty
عُنْف	violence
أَعْمال العُنْف	acts of violence
نَبْذ العُنْف	renunciation of violence
عَمَليّة اِنْتِحاريّة	suicide operation
سَيّارة مُفَخَّخة	car bomb (lit. booby-trapped car)
مَقْتَل	murder, killing
قَطْع الرَأْس	beheading
إصابة، ـات	injury
عُنْصُريّة	racism
إرْهاب	terrorism
تَجَسُّس	espionage
خيانة	treason
أَعْمال التَخْريب	acts of sabotage
جَريمة القَتْل	homicide
مَقْتَل بِالرَصاص	(fatal) shooting
سَرِقة / سِرْقة، ـات	burglary, theft
تَهْريب البَشَر	people trafficking
مُحاوَلة اِنْقِلابيّة	attempted coup

اِنْقِلاب أَبْيَض	bloodless coup
حالة الطَوارِئ	state of emergency
مُحاوَلة اِغْتِيال	assassination attempt
مُهاتَرة	abuse, insult
مُمارَسات فاسِدة	corrupt practices
غِشّ	fraud
تَهَرُّب مِن الضَرائِب	tax evasion
عَمَليات اِحْتِيال	scams
فَضيحة، فَضائِح	scandal
مُؤامَرة	conspiracy
عِصْيان مَدَنيّ	civil disobedience
اِحْتِجاج، ـات	protest
تَهْديد، ـات	threat
تحَدٍّ، تَحَدّيات	challenge
اِسْتِفْزاز، ـات	provocation
مُظاهَرة، ـات	demonstration
اِشْتِباك، ـات	clash, scuffle
شَغَب، أَحْداث شَغَب	riot
إضْراب عَن الطَعام	hunger strike
اِعْتِصام	sit-in
مُخَدِّرات	drugs
مَسْرُوقات	stolen goods

عَمالة الأطْفال	child labour
تَحْقيق جِنائيّ، ‑ات جِنائيّة	criminal investigation
إنْحِراف	delinquency
مَشْرُوعيّة	legality
تَرْخيص، تَراخيص	permit, licence
تَفْويض، ‑ات	power of attorney
كامِل الأهْليّة	legally competent
عَديم الأهْليّة	legally incompetent
قانونيّ \ شَرْعيّ	legal
غَيْر قانونيّ \ غَيْر شَرْعيّ	illegal
جِنائيّ	criminal (adj.)
مُسَلَّح	armed
غَيْر مُسَلَّح	unarmed
عِقابيّ	punitive, penal
مُفْتَرَض	alleged
بَريء، أبْرياء	innocent
مُذْنِب، ‑ون	guilty
جَلْسة مَحْكَمة	court hearing
رَأْي يُعَدّ غَيْر مُلْزِم	non-binding opinion
إرْتَكَب	to commit, perpetrate
إتَّهَم ه بـ	to accuse s.o. of s.t.
وَجَّه اتِّهامات ضِدّ	to press charges against

اِسْتَدْعى	to summon
حاكَم	to try
قاضَى	to prosecute
اِسْتَجْوَب	to interrogate, examine
حَقَّق	to verify, investigate
أدان يُدين إدانة ه بِ	to convict s.o. of s.t.
اِسْتَذْنَب	to find guilty
أَبْرَأ	to acquit
عَفا يعفو عَفْو	to pardon
أَفْرَج عَن	to release
طعن يطعَن طَعْن في	to contest
اِسْتَأْنَف	to appeal
اِعْتَرَف بِ	to confess, admit
عاقَب	to punish
صادَر	to confiscate
غَرَّم	to fine
رفع يرفَع رَفْع دَعْوَى عَلَى	to sue
حكم يحكُم حُكُم عَلَيْهِ بالإِعْدام	to sentence s.o. to death
حكم عَلَيْهِ بِالسِجْنِ المُؤَبَّد	to sentence s.o. to life imprisonment
أَعْدَم	to execute
شنق يشنُق شَنْق	to hang

عَذَّب	to torture
أَوْقَف \ وَقَّف	to stop, restrain
اِعْتَقَل	to arrest
قبض يقبِض قَبْض على	"
أَلْقَى القَبْض عَلَى	"
اِحْتَجَز	to detain
سجَن يسجُن سَجْن	to imprison
أساء المُعامَلة	to mistreat
أَبْعَد	to deport
طرد يطرُد طَرْد	to expel
نفَى ينفي نَفْي	to exile
عاش يَعيش عَيْش في المَنْفَى	to live in exile
اِرْتَكَب	to commit (a crime)
وضع يَضِع وَضْع في حال تَأَهُّب قُصْوَى	to put on red alert
فرض يفرُض فَرْض حَظْرَ التَجَوُّل	to impose a curfew
فرض يفرُض فَرْض الحُكْم العُرْفِيّ	to impose martial law
جَمَّد الأمْوال	to freeze assets
قَنَّن	to legalise
أَعْلَن مَسْؤوليَّتَه عَن	to claim/declare one's responsibility for

دعا يَدْعو دَعْوة إلَى إضْراب	to call a strike
اِحْتَجّ عَلَى	to protest against
تَظاهَر	to demonstrate
ناهَض	to resist, oppose
تَصاعَد	to escalate (v.i.)
تَلاءَم مَع	to comply with
خالَف القانون	to break the law
اِنْتَهَك	to violate, infringe
تَوَرَّط في	to be involved in
هَدَّد ه ب	to threaten s.o. with s.t.
اِخْتَطَف	to take hostage, abduct
هَرَّب	to smuggle
سرق يسرِق سَرِقة	to loot
قتل يقتُل قَتْل	to murder
اِغْتال	to assassinate
خطِف يخطَف خَطْف	to hijack
اِغْتَصَب	to rape
اِبْتَزّ	to blackmail
اِخْتَلَس	to embezzle
اِحْتال	to defraud

8. DISASTER & AID

أَزْمة، أَزَمات	crisis
كارِثة، كَوارِث	disaster, catastrophe
طارِئة، طَوارِئ	emergency
حالة التَأَهُّب القُصْوَى	state of high alert
مَأْساة، مآسٍ	tragedy
مَجاعة	famine
جَفاف	drought
سُوْء التَغْذية	malnutrition
فَظاعة، فَظائِع	atrocity
زِلْزال، زَلازِل	earthquake
هَزّة أَرْضيّة، ـات أَرْضيّة	earth tremor, seismic shock
بِمِقْياس ريخْتَر	on the Richter scale
فَيَضان، ـات	flood
سَيْل، سُيول	"
إعْصار، ـات	hurricane
تسونامي	tsunami
سَحابة رَماد	ash cloud
بُرْكان، بَراكين	volcano
تَسَرُّب نَفْطيّ	oil slick
كارِثة نَوَويّة	nuclear disaster

اِنْصِهار نَوَويّ	nuclear meltdown
تَسَرُّب نَوَويّ	nuclear leak
إشْعاع نَوَويّ	nuclear radiation
مُخَلَّفات سامّة	toxic waste
تَحَطُّم طائِرة	plane crash
حادِث، حَوادِث	accident
اِنْهِيار طينيّ، ـات طينيّة	mudslide
حَريق، حَرائِق	fire
خَسائِر بَشَريّة	human loss (Arabic pl.)
أضْرار مادّيّة	material damage (Arabic pl.)
حُزْن	sorrow, distress
اِكْتِئاب \ إحْباط \ وُجوم	depression
قَلَق	anxiety
حاجة ماسّة إلَى	pressing need for
مُعَدَّل الوَفَيات	mortality rate
مُعَدَّل المَواليد	birth rate
العالَم الثالِث	the third world
دُوَل مُتَخَلِّفة	developing (lit. backward) countries
أحْياء فَقيرة	slums
لاجِئ، ـون	refugee
طالِب اللُّجوء، طالِبو اللُّجوء	asylum seeker

مُهاجِر، ‑ون	immigrant
جائِع، جِياع	starving (person)
مُتَشَرِّد، ‑ون	homeless (person)
مَعُونة \ إغاثة	aid
مُساعَدات	aid, help (Arabic pl.)
مُساعَدات عاجِلة	emergency aid
مُساعَدات غِذائيّة	food aid
مُساعَدات فَنّيّة	technical aid
مُساعَدات ماليّة	financial aid
مُساعَدات تَنْمويّة	development aid
دَعْم	support
إعانات الدَوْلة	state handouts
مِنْحة، مِنَح	grant
عَطاء، أَعْطِية	gift
سَخاء	generosity
إلْغاء الدُيون	debt cancellation
عامِل الإغاثة، عُمّال الإغاثة	aid worker
مُتَطَوِّع، ‑ون	volunteer
هَيْئة المَعُونة	aid/relief organisation
مُنَظَّمة طَوْعيّة	voluntary organisation
مُنَظَّمة خَيريّة	charity
دَوْلة الرَفاه	the welfare state

ضَمان اِجْتِماعيّ social security

هَيْئة الصَليبِ الأَحْمَر the Red Cross

هَيْئة الهِلالِ الأَحْمَر the Red Crescent

جَماعة السَّلام الأَخْضَر Greenpeace

وِكالة إغاثة اللاجِئين للأُمَم المُتَّحِدة UNRWA (United Nations Relief and Works Agency)

بَرْنامِج الأُمَم المُتَّحِدة الإنمائيّ UNDP (United Nations Development Programme)

البَنْك الدُوَليّ لِلإنْشاء والتَعْمير IBRD (International Bank for Reconstruction and Development)

مُنَظَّمة الصِحّة العالَميّة WHO (World Health Organization)

بَرْنامِج الأَغْذية العالَميّ WFP (World Food Programme)

الصُنْدوق العالَميّ لِلطَبيعة WWF (Worldwide Fund For Nature)

مُنَظَّمة غَيْر حُكوميّة NGO (non-governmental organisation)

مُنَظَّمة أَطِبّاء بِلا حُدود MSF (Médecins Sans Frontières)

قافِلة الأَغْذية food convoy

شاحِنة، ـات lorry, truck

خَيْمة، ـات \ خِيام tent

هِجْرة immigration

تَخْفيض عَدَدِ السُكَّان	depopulation
اِنْقِراض	extinction
إزالة الغابات	deforestation
تَآكُل	erosion
تَغَيُّر مُناخيّ	climate change
اِحْتِباس حَراريّ	global warming
تَلَوُّث	pollution
أمْطار سَوْداء	black rain
حِماية البيئة	environmental protection
طَبَقة الأُوزون	ozone hole
اِنْبِعاثات كاربونيّة	carbon emissions
أُمّيّة	illiteracy
وَباء، أَوْبِئة	epidemic
الأيْدز	AIDS
فَقْر	poverty
تَخْريب	devastation
اِضْطِرابات	disruption (Arabic pl.)
شَلَل	paralysis
إعادة الإسْكان	resettlement
إجْلاء	evacuation
إعادة الإعْمار	reconstruction
تَخْطيط مَدَنيّ	urban planning

رَيّ	irrigation
تَنْقية المِياه	water purification
تَحْلية المِياه	desalination
لَقاح	vaccine
تَنْظيم الأُسْرة	family planning
عاجِل	urgent
تَحْتَ خَطِّ الفَقْر	below the poverty line
طارِئ	emergency (adj.)
تَطْويريّ	developmental
إنْسانيّ	humanitarian
طَوْعيّ	voluntary
تَنَقَّل	to migrate, roam
هاجَر	to emigrate
تَدَفَّق	to pour into
فرّ يِفِرّ فَرّ \ فِرار	to flee
أَجْلَى	to evacuate
تَعَرَّض لِ	to be exposed to
أَتْلَف	to ruin, damage, destroy
دفن، يدفِن، دَفْن	to bury
لَقَّح	to vaccinate
أَعْلَن ه مِنْطَقة مُتَضَرِّرة / مَنْكُوبة	to proclaim s.t. a disaster area

خَرَّب   to devastate, lay waste to

تَفاقَم   to become critical

اِنْقَرَض   to become extinct

INDEX

Printed and bound by CPI Group (UK) Ltd, Croydon, CR0 4YY

14/11/2024

01788502-0002